D1710771

# What Was It Like, Mr. Emperor?

Life in China's Forbidden City

China
INSTITUTE

CnC 設計及文化研究工作室
DESIGN AND CULTURAL
STUDIES WORKSHOP

何 鴻 毅 家 族 基 金
THE ROBERT H. N. HO
FAMILY FOUNDATION

# TABLE OF CONTENTS

**WHEN MY FATHER,** Robert H. N. Ho, decided to establish a family foundation to support Chinese culture and Buddhist philosophy, it was a modest beginning to facing a formidable challenge: how to preserve and make more accessible globally the treasure trove which is embodied in over 5,000 years of Chinese history and culture. Since 2005, The Robert H. N. Ho Family Foundation, based in Hong Kong, has been active around the world, supporting cultural projects and academic exchange in collaboration with museums, galleries, universities, artists, curators, and scholars. Education has been a common thread running through all of our foundation's work, especially the development of cultural awareness amongst the emerging generation of young Chinese who, not unlike their counterparts around the world, have been swept away by the compelling amusements of the Internet and 21st century youth culture.

Chinese parents, like parents around the world, are concerned that their children might lose their connection with their cultural roots. It was with that in mind that our foundation decided to support Mr. Chiu Kwong-chiu and his team at Design and Cultural Studies Workshop in Hong Kong, to develop a series of books, **We All Live in the Forbidden City,** using the theme of Beijing's ancient palace as a platform to educate young people about many important aspects of Chinese history and culture. The books and related outreach activities have proved to be a popular and engaging way to inform as well as "edutain."

Having supported these publications both in Hong Kong (published in traditional Chinese characters) and in mainland China (published in simplified Chinese characters), it is only natural that we make these award-winning books more widely available to an English language audience.

As urban areas in North America, Europe, and the Antipodes become increasingly multi-cultural, so has our world become smaller with the increasing interdependence, economic and otherwise, between East and West. It is crucially important that young people learn more not just about their own culture, but also explore other cultures as well. My family and I hope this wonderful English language version, developed in collaboration with China Institute in America and Tuttle Publishing, will help bridge the gap between East and West, and continue to inform and entertain young people around the world.

**Robert Yau Chung Ho**
Chairman
The Robert H. N. Ho Family Foundation

**THE ANCIENTS BELIEVED** that the star of **Ziwei,** also known as Polaris, never changed its position. They believed that the star was enclosed by a purple bright constellation and that it was the home of the Great Imperial Ruler of Heaven. In China, the emperor was thought to be the son of the Great Imperial Ruler of Heaven, and this was how his palace came to be called the Purple Forbidden City.

In 1421 the third Ming dynasty emperor, Yongle, working with the collective power of the nation, finished construction on this majestic palace in Beijing. The Forbidden City occupies a total area of 720,000 square meters. Flanking its four sides are colossal city walls and a broad palace moat. Together these protect a sprawling landscape of towers, halls, and pavilions, made up of red bricks and golden roof tiles.

For almost 600 years, the Forbidden City was the home of the Chinese emperor. It contained a stupendous amount of masterpieces and rare treasures, which were handed down from generation to generation. Countless imperial and historical events occurred here through the vicissitudes of time. Eventually, the Chinese Revolution of 1911 overthrew the imperial system that had ruled China for thousands of years. Then, in October of 1925, the Palace Museum was established on the grounds of the existing palace. On that day, the Forbidden City opened its doors to the public and, ever since, the palace has taken on the role of a spiritual home and cultural heritage site for everyone to enjoy.

Today, the Palace Museum is the world's largest and most well preserved royal architectural complex. Around 1,800,000 pieces of historical artifacts are stored inside. Every year, it welcomes tens of millions of visitors, as its allure and splendor increasingly attract greater attention from around the globe.

The Hong Kong-based scholar Mr. Chiu Kwong-chiu is someone who has planted his roots in the Forbidden City. He and his team, the Design and Cultural Studies Workshop, research and interpret the subject matter deeply and earnestly. Mr. Chiu's passion for the Forbidden City is evident in all of his books, from **The Grand Forbidden City – The Imperial Axis** to **The Twelve Beauties** to this current series, **We All Live in the Forbidden City,** which has been designed for a younger audience. Especially in this series of illustrative books, Mr. Chiu's unique perspective, along with the dynamic use of language and drawings, enliven and animate the Forbidden City, a place that is austere and lofty in nature. Through these books, you will experience the palace's grandeur, but you will also find delight in its refined elegance. In a joyful manner, everything that is unique about the Forbidden City comes to life.

It made me very happy to learn that the English editions of several books from **We All Live in the Forbidden City** would be published in New York. By way of these books, I hope that the children in North America will find themselves being transported on a colorful journey to the Forbidden City, as they develop their understanding of Chinese history and culture.

I wish everyone an exciting voyage!

**Shan Jixiang**
Director
The Palace Museum

## Foreword

### Dear Mr. Emperor:

We have heard of the magnificence and wisdom with which you ruled over China. Your civilian and military staffs, and the people saw that, with the enormous power and authority you possessed, you were able to enjoy all the glory and luxury there is in life. It seems as if you must have been the greatest and happiest man on earth! Yet there were times it seemed that all you cared about was enjoying the good life, leading a life of pleasure and neglecting your royal duties.

We realize that you no longer rule China, and that the last emperor – the one closest to us in time – departed the Forbidden City almost a century ago. To hear that he ascended the throne when he was only 3 years old – how incredible! What a pity that there were no televisions or smart phones back then to record anything.

If only we could hear you utter one sound, we might get to know a little more about you. So tell us the truth, Mr. Emperor: Were you really a dragon reincarnated? Were you happy? Would you sometimes be hurt and sad? What was your favorite food? Did you have to go to school? Did you have holidays? Would you be punished for doing something wrong?

**So, in short, what exactly was your life like Mr. Emperor?**

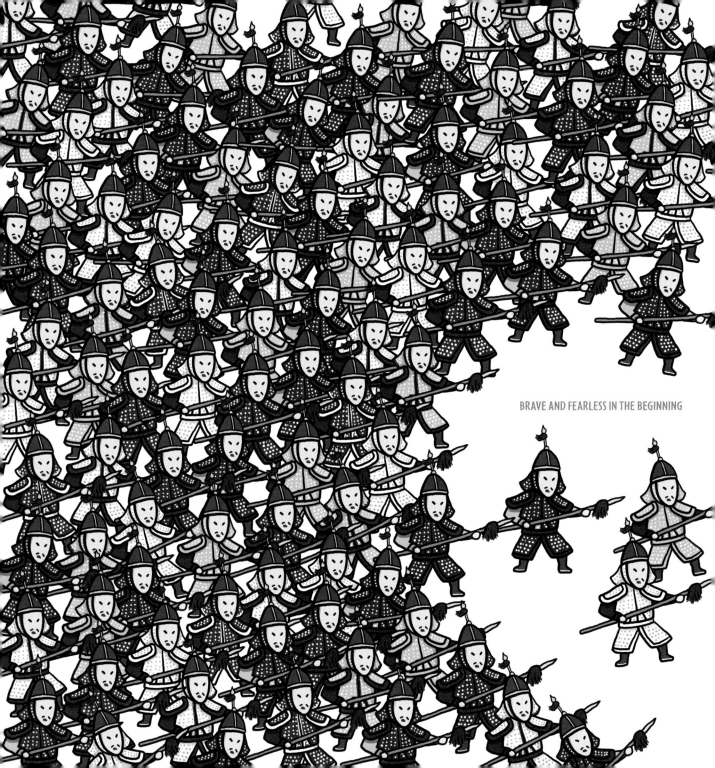

BRAVE AND FEARLESS IN THE BEGINNING

The emperor is supremely noble. Common people, stay away!

EUNUCH

Numerous people would have liked to be the emperor, but even more wanted to hurt him. In China's history almost 1/3 of the emperors were murdered. Therefore tight security was important for protecting him. During the Qing dynasty (1644-1911), the imperial military guards were banner soldiers, from the Eight Banners. The Eight Banners were administrative and military units developed by the Manchus, the people that established the Qing dynasty. These young imperial guards, at the same time as they protected the emperor, were being groomed and trained to be future officials of the court. These imperial guards were known for their bravery at the beginning of the Qing dynasty, but became sloppy in their duties toward the end.

LATER THEY GOT SLOPPY.

11

NU WA

FU XI

SHEN NONG

OX HEAD!

BODY OF SNAKE!

BODY OF SNAKE!

## The Three Legendary Sovereigns of China...

According to legend, China's earliest three rulers emerged before the Xia dynasty (4000–2500 BC). They had great wisdom and created many ideas and objects that brought prosperity and happiness to the people of the land. Nu Wa, the Goddess of Creation, holds a circular compass. Fu Xi, God of Fire, has a carpenter's square, symbol of proper conduct. Shen Nong, God of Agriculture, holds a bouquet of medicinal herbs. Nu Wa and Fu Xi taught the people law and order. Shen Nong taught them farming and how to practice medicine.

EMPEROR KU  EMPEROR ZHUAN XU  HUANGDI
THE YELLOW EMPEROR

EMPEROR SHUN  EMPEROR YAO

## And the Five Legendary Emperors

And then there were the Five Legendary Emperors. More than 4,000 years ago, in a tribe named Ji there was Huangdi, who led his people into many battles with a tribe named Jiang, led by Emperor Yan. Huangdi and his tribe won an important battle, but soon after, the victors united with the defeated, and all the people thereafter called themselves the "descendants of Yan and Huang." This phrase now refers to the Chinese people. Huangdi, or the Yellow Emperor, passed his position of leadership down four generations. These five chiefs ruled the land in peace and prosperity. This period was fondly remembered as the golden days of ancient China. The five chiefs went on to be known as the Five Legendary Emperors.

**In the year 200 BC, Yingzheng of the Qin unified the divided states of China.**

He thought his accomplishments topped the Three Legendary Sovereigns and the Five Legendary Emperors, and so he proclaimed himself the "First Emperor" – Qin Shi Huangdi.

The emergence of the word "emperor" (huangdi) in China signifies that the land of China was no longer chaotically divided among many states led by many chiefs. It had become one unified nation ruled by one man – the emperor and his descendants. The emperor's edicts applied to every corner and to every person on the land. None could challenge or defy them.

**The First Emperor**

Officially, there have been 210 emperors in China, from the first emperor of the Qin dynasty, Qin Shi Huangdi, to the last emperor of the Qing dynasty, Puyi. There was one female emperor, Wu Zetian of the Tang dynasty (618-907). Every one of these emperors, especially the ones who founded their own dynasties, did their best to convince their citizens that they were the true descendants of Heaven. It was thought that Heaven bestowed upon them the power to rule and whoever could claim the title of "Son of Heaven" would have the authority to rule over the people. The emperor would be addressed in solemn reverence as "His Majesty." During the imperial era in China, the emperor was the pivotal character and symbol of the nation. This entitled him to live in the grandest and most luxurious buildings: the imperial palaces.

**The emperor is truly the Son of Heaven.**

# How The Emperors Addressed Themselves

**Gua Ren
(I, the only Ruler)**

EMPEROR

OH, HOW LONESOME!

Gua Ren ("Person who lacks virtue") was the humble title used by rulers and kings during the "Spring and Autumn" and "Warring States" periods of the Eastern Zhou dynasty (770–476 BC). The phrase means "I, the only Ruler," in English.

OH, HOW FORLORN!

Zhen
(I, the Ruler)

THE EMPRESS AND IMPERIAL CONSORTS

GEE-WHIZ! SO HUMBLE AND INSIGNIFICANT!

The character pronounced Zhen means "I, or me." Beginning with the First Emperor of the Qin dynasty (221-206 BC), this was the character used by emperors to refer to themselves.

Ai Jia
(I, the Grief-Ridden Empress)

THE EMPEROR HAS PASSED AWAY.
OH, WOE IS ME!

EMPRESS DOWAGER

It wasn't until after the emperor had passed away that the empress, now the empress dowager, could address herself as Ai Jia, or the grief-ridden empress.

OH, MY...

I, THE
SLAVE

IMPERIAL CONSORTS

I, THE
UNWORTHY
CONCUBINE...

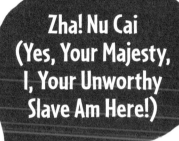

IMPORTANT COURT OFFICIALS

DECLARING THEIR UNWORTHY STATUS

Even the imperial family was miserable. Could you imagine what life was like for the common people? The emperor rules a nation. He has the most power. A good ruler brought peace, union, and stability to his people, so that they would have a happy life. Under an incompetent ruler, the people's quality of life would decline.

Generally speaking, the founding emperors of dynasties were bright and competent. But the same could not always be said about the emperors who followed. Because of the importance of an emperor to the country, every citizen was filled with high EXPECTATIONS for him.

**Yes, I am willing!**

BRILLIANT AND COURAGEOUS

BENEVOLENT AND KIND

PREGNANT IMPERIAL CONSORTS

Living in the inner palace, the imperial consorts focused their energy on how to better serve the emperor. They wanted to give birth to his children so as to sustain the royal line and strengthen the imperial family. As a result, every imperial concubine had a fervent wish to beat the others in bringing him children. Whoever gave birth to an emperor's child would see her status and rank rise. With a newborn child, a consort could move to more luxurious quarters in the palace with more servants at her disposal. What's more, three months before the baby was born, imperial medical staff members would look after her night and day, and she would receive 50% more in her monthly allowance for dining and drinking.

Even before the emperor was born, the citizens had high expectations for him.

I'm Quite Stressed Out.

MEDICINAL SOUP FOR
AN EARLY DELIVERY

## How Emperor Xianfeng of the Qing Dynasty Was Born Early

In the fifth lunar month of the tenth year of Emperor Daoguang's reign (June 1830), two Imperial Consorts named Perfection and Auspicious were both expecting a baby. It was predicted that Auspicious would give birth to her child before Perfection. It is rumored that this drove the desperate Perfection to drink an herbal medicinal soup every day to quicken the delivery. The result of this birthing competition was that Perfection delivered a baby boy six days before Auspicious. This boy was the fourth prince. He later ascended the throne as Emperor Xianfeng. However, due to his premature birth, Xianfeng had poor health. He was plagued by many illnesses and died at the early age of 31.

A baby fared best if he was born a prince. He would have the chance to become emperor. But if the baby were a princess, her life would be very different. She would have to marry young (the youngest were 10 years old!) and would often be married off to someone in a distant land. Most of the princesses led a short life, living to an average age of twenty-two.

Though the first-born, I have few opportunities in life.

I'm Lucky

PRINCESS

PRINCE

PRINCE

PRINCE

PRINCE

SACHIMA
(MANCHU PASTRY)

PRINCE

PRINCESS

## Imperial Allowances

Set allowances for the princes, princesses, sons and daughters of princes and princesses, and grandchildren of princes and princesses were as follows:

10 taels of silver per month after a prince is born

50 taels of silver a month once a prince begins school

500 taels of silver a month after a prince marries

900 taels of silver a year on the prince's birthday, after he's married

10 taels of silver a month after a princess is one month old

40 taels of silver a month after a princess turns six

200 taels of silver a month starting the day after the son of a prince marries

100 taels of silver a month starting the day after the grandson of a prince marries

Usually, before the Qing dynasty, only the empress's eldest prince or eldest grandson would be heir to the throne. In this great Qing dynasty of ours, however, every prince has the chance of becoming emperor.

## Key Manchurian Terms

**Huang A Ma**
Emperor, my father

**Huang E Niang**
Empress, my mother

**A Ge**
Royal Prince

**Ge Ge**
Royal Princess

**Mo Mo**
Wet Nurse

**Su La**
Male Servant

**Aisin** Golden
**Aisin-Gioro** Last Name of the Qing Imperial Family

**A Qi Na** Dog

Emperor Yongzheng (r.1723–1736) issued an imperial edict to have his eighth younger brother's name changed to A Qi Na (Dog). He also ordered that he be banished from the imperial family, just like an unwanted dog.

**Sachima**
traditional Manchurian pastry similar to a Rice Krispies treat

27

One of the strict imperial family rules said that the prince had to be separated from his mother at a young age. Otherwise the relationship between the prince and his mother might become so close as to dangerously empower the maternal family. This could then weaken the strength of the paternal (emperor's) family.

Finally the prince is born. But he must be separated from his mom, leaving him in care to the wet nurse.

**Here's a toy, your Highness!**

TOY

EUNUCH

EUNUCH

TOY

From the time a prince was born until he became an adult, the people closest to him were not his family members. Instead, they were a group of eunuchs who were not blood relations. A prince or princess did have a great number of toys though, some of which were given to them by an empress dowager or other noblewoman. Other toys were given to them by eunuchs and imperial chambermaids.

TOY

## Diligence (Classroom Culture in the Qing Palace)

As any of the princes could become emperor, they all received a strict and rigorous education.

Princes started their schooling at the age of six. Young as they were, they had to study Confucian classics and history, including The Five Classics, Records of the Grand Historian, Book of Han, Book of Songs, and others. To prepare them for a life in politics, different languages were taught to them, including Chinese, Mongolian, Manchu, and later English. So that they could protect and defend the country, princes also received training in the martial arts and physical exercise, including combined horse riding and archery. It was hoped that through all this training the princes would become ideal emperors, steeped in both scholarly subjects and military affairs.

30

## Schedule for the Prince's Daily Studies (With Only Five Holidays a Year!)

Before sunrise, a prince would wake up and go to school. Classes ran from 5:00 in the morning until 3:00 in the afternoon, at least ten hours a day, seven days a week. The five holidays he got off were New Year's Day, the Dragon Boat Festival, the Mid-Autumn Festival, the Emperor's Birthday, and the prince's own birthday. A prince had to study even on New Year's Eve. In comparison, the number of holidays in a year for today's students is equivalent to the number of holidays a Manchu prince would have in 37 years!

## School Days

Emperor Qianlong, father of Emperor Jiaqing, had a very long life.
Consequently, Jiaqing ended up studying at school for over 30 years!
He studied even longer than PhD students today.

## Martial Arts

The Manchus were a nomadic people who were experts on horseback. They placed high importance on military prowess. After dinner every evening, the prince had to attend a class for military physical education, receiving training in horsemanship, archery and other military arts from masters of the Manchu and Mongol aristocracy.

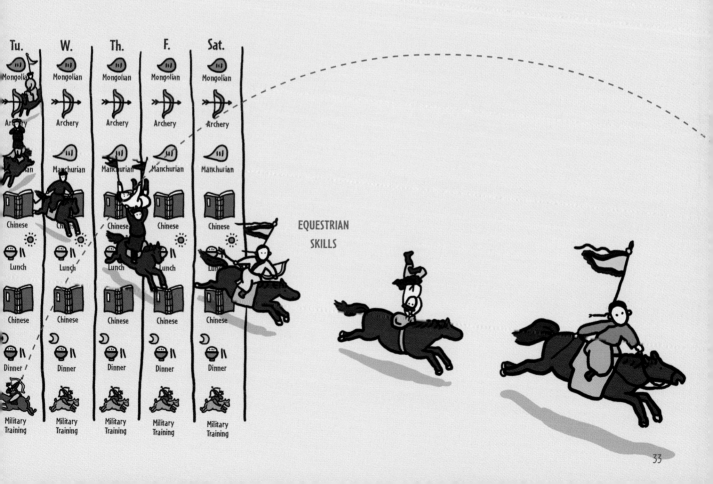

EQUESTRIAN
SKILLS

SECOND PRINCE MINNING

INSURGENTS OF THE
WHITE LOTUS SECT

Fighting with
distinguished skill.
Confidently defeating
his opponents.

INSURGENTS OF THE
WHITE LOTUS SECT

In 1813, an insurgent leader named Lin Qing led 200 fanatics of the White Lotus sect into the Forbidden City. At the time Emperor Jiaqing was at his summer retreat in Chengde, northeast of Beijing. Lin and his army managed to fight through two gates, aided by some high-ranking eunuchs. He did this with the aim of "toppling the Manchu monarch and restoring the Ming dynasty, by the divine order of Heaven."

In command of imperial soldiers in the palace, Second Prince Minning put up a fierce battle of resistance against the rebels. After two days of battle, the rebels were defeated and their leader Lin Qing was executed. Afterwards, arrowheads remained stuck in the plaque above the Gate of Thriving Imperial Clan. Greatly shaken by the insurgence, Emperor Jiaqing issued an imperial edict not to remove the arrowheads as a reminder of this incident. Yet Emperor Jiaqing was also impressed and pleased by the calm way in which Prince Minning defeated the insurgents and showered high praises on him. Minning later succeeded Jiaqing as Emperor Daoguang, the sixth emperor of the Qing dynasty.

The throne was passed down from generation to generation, and typically the emperor chose the prince that would succeed him on his deathbed. Understandably, fierce rivalries among the princes for the emperor's favor were unavoidable. Therefore, it was a challenging decision for an emperor to decide which prince would succeed him.

## An Imperial Secret Revealed

To prevent the fierce (sometimes bloody) rivalry among the princes to succeed the emperor to the throne, Emperor Yongzheng came up with a solution known as the "Box with the Name of the Heir Apparent." The emperor would secretly issue two copies of an imperial edict that would name the prince who was his heir apparent. One copy was to be carried by the emperor at all times and the other was to be placed inside the "Box with the Name of the Heir Apparent," which was then safely and discreetly hidden behind a plaque in the Hall of Heavenly Purity in the Forbidden City, on which the words "Upright and Pure in Mind" were written. When the emperor passed on, a group of the most prominent ministers and senior relatives would take out the box. The two edicts would be compared and only then was the great secret revealed: the name of the new emperor.

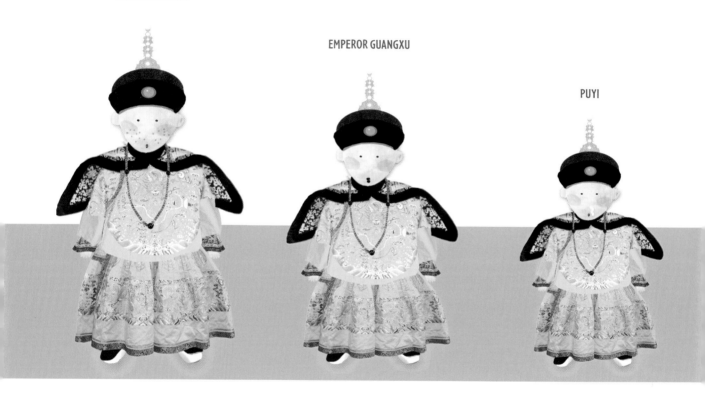

EMPEROR KANGXI

EMPEROR GUANGXU

PUYI

During the Qing dynasty, each emperor had a ceremony, held at the Hall of Supreme Harmony in the Forbidden City, to commemorate the beginning of his rule. Emperor Shunzhi had his crowning ceremony when he was 6, and received his ceremony for starting to rule at 14. Crowned at 8, Emperor Kangxi received his ceremony to mark the beginning of his rule when he turned 14. Emperor Guangxu ascended to the throne when he was 4, but did not receive his ceremony to start ruling until he was 19. The last emperor crowned was Puyi, at the young age of 3.

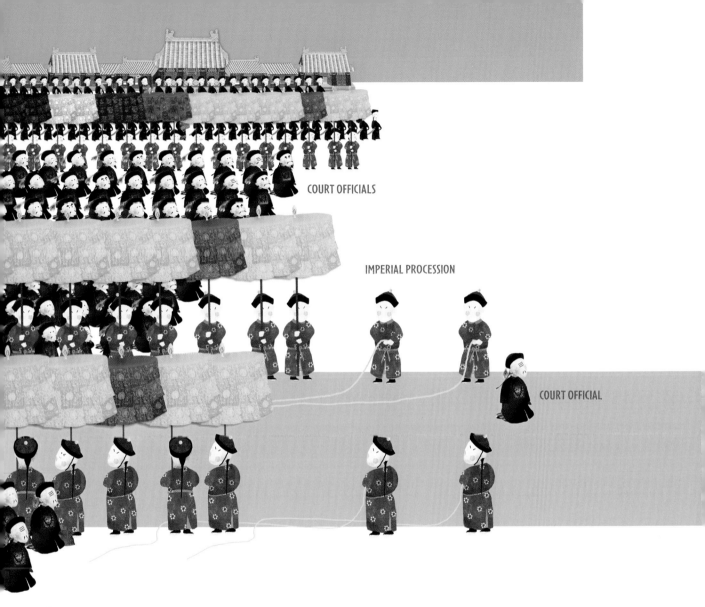

COURT OFFICIALS

IMPERIAL PROCESSION

COURT OFFICIAL

COURT OFFICIALS

# THE EMPEROR SPEAKS

The imperial family consisted of all those even distantly related to the emperor. It was like a large tree where the emperor was the trunk and the other imperial relatives were the leaves and branches. The taller and sturdier the trunk, the more the branches and leaves would flourish. The emperor and the imperial family were served by a huge staff of eunuchs and palace maids. Under them were servants in charge of miscellaneous chores and a brigade of soldiers whose duty it was to protect the emperor and the imperial family.

**The Imperial Family Tree**

What a Good
Role Model

FILIAL AND HONORABLE

## Civilian and Military Officials

Except for aristocrats or the emperor's relatives, court officials
were usually appointed through recommendations by local
officials. Starting in the Han dynasty (206 BC–220 AD), local
government officials would recommend scholars who were
both filial (respectful to their elders) and honorable to serve as
officials. The practice was known as "Recommending the Filial
and the Honorable."

Greetings, Teacher!

STUDYING IS THE ONLY NOBLE THING TO DO IN LIFE.

The most direct way for a scholar to rise through the ranks and serve in the court was through studying and passing a series of examinations up to the highest imperial examination. With the passing of these examinations he first would become a county scholar, a provincial scholar, and then a national scholar, ultimately becoming an imperial first-ranking scholar. A scholar had to dedicate his life to serving the country, in turn bringing glory and pride to his family and ancestors. Due to the fact that many rulers in the history of China placed great emphasis on study, the court always had more scholars than military men on staff.

## Military Officials

Being able to shoot a bow and arrow while on horseback was an important skill for the Manchus. In order not to neglect or forget this tradition of their ancestors, military officials had to practice their drills daily. Young men of Manchu descent were advised not to forget nor disregard this tradition. (At least this was true at the beginning of the Qing dynasty.) Even princes had to attend daily military physical education classes: a most rigorous requirement.

Imperial chefs, handy with sharp objects, were also on the military's staff.

| FIRST RANK: | SECOND RANK: | THIRD RANK: | FOURTH RANK: | FIFTH RANK: |
|---|---|---|---|---|
| MANCHURIAN CRANE | GOLDEN PHEASANT | PEACOCK | WILD GOOSE | SILVER PHEASANT |

| SIXTH RANK: | SEVENTH RANK: | | EIGHTH RANK: | NINTH RANK: |
|---|---|---|---|---|
| LESSER EGRET | MANDARIN DUCK | | QUAIL | PARADISE FLYCATCHER |

## Civil Official

**FIRST RANK:**
QILIN

**SECOND RANK:**
LION

**THIRD RANK:**
LEOPARD

**FOURTH RANK:**
TIGER

**FIFTH RANK:**
BEAR

**SIXTH RANK:**
PANTHER

**SEVENTH & EIGHTH RANKS:**
RHINOCEROS

**NINTH RANK:**
SEA HORSE

Military Official

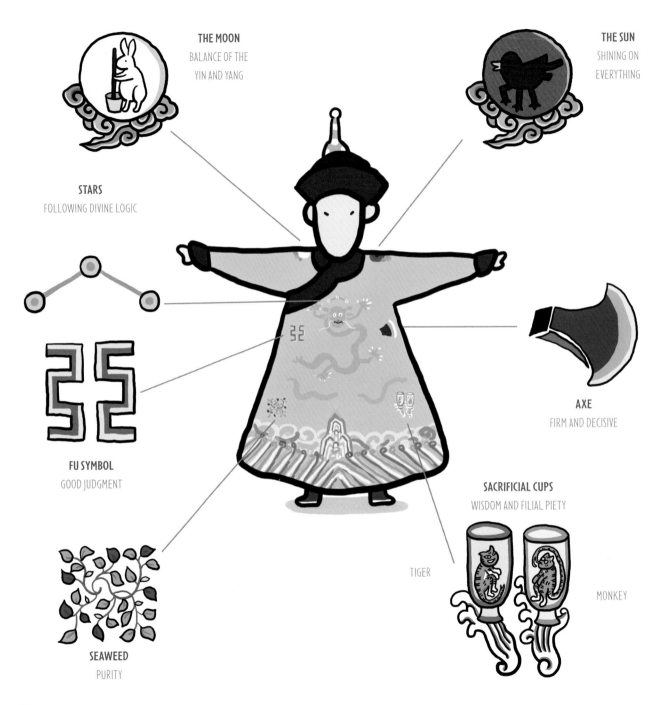

**THE MOON**
BALANCE OF THE
YIN AND YANG

**THE SUN**
SHINING ON
EVERYTHING

**STARS**
FOLLOWING DIVINE LOGIC

**AXE**
FIRM AND DECISIVE

**FU SYMBOL**
GOOD JUDGMENT

**SACRIFICIAL CUPS**
WISDOM AND FILIAL PIETY

TIGER

MONKEY

**SEAWEED**
PURITY

**DRAGON**
GRACE UNDER PRESSURE

**MOUNTAIN**
STABILITY

**FIRE**
HONESTY

**PHEASANT**
LITERARY BRILLIANCE

## The Emperor's Imperial Court Robe:
## 12 Emblems Representing the 12 Virtues

These 12 emblems were embroidered on the imperial robe, a tradition
that was started during the Zhou dynasty (1046–256 BC). The traditional
rule stated that, as the Son of Heaven, the emperor had to wear a robe
with this design. The 12 emblems represented the most important
virtues contained in the supreme powers held by the emperor.

**GRAIN**
PROSPERITY

## National Affairs (In the Outer Court)
## Family Affairs (In the Inner Court)

The Chinese phrase "Family and Country" refers to an ideal way that a ruler should manage his affairs. What this phrase means is that one must first improve oneself before one can start a happy family. One must then be able to manage a happy family before one can rule an entire nation.

The importance of this idea can be seen in the construction of the Forbidden City. The Outer Court was where the emperor tended to national affairs. The Inner Court was the home of the emperor, where he had to look after the harmony of his family.

## The Empress Really Rules the Inner Court

While the emperor had to rule the nation, his wife, the empress, had to serve as the nation's "mother," representing ideal virtues of refinement and good manners. Her duties were to manage the affairs in the Inner Court, where the imperial family lived, so the emperor did not have to worry about domestic problems.

In imperial China the emperors had many imperial consorts, and they were separated into eight ranks. In the Qing dynasty, most of the consorts came from the Eight Banners noble families.

EMPRESS

IMPERIAL MAIDS

**The Eight Ranks of Imperial Consorts during the Qing dynasty:**

1 Empress, with 10 maids

1 Imperial Noble Consort, with 8 maids

2 Noble Consorts, with 8 maids each

4 Consorts, with 6 maids each

6 Imperial Concubines, with 6 maids each

An unlimited number of Noble Ladies, with 4 maids each

An unlimited number of First Class Female Attendants, with 3 maids each

An unlimited number of Second Class Female Attendants, with 2 maids each

The number of maids in the palace would not exceed 2,000.

**Our Queen Mother, the Empress**

EUNUCHS

9,000 IMPERIAL MAIDS

A NOISY GROUP

FORBIDDEN TO
LEAVE THE PALACE

MING IMPERIAL MAIDS

INNER COURT DURING
THE MING DYNASTY

During the Qing dynasty, the imperial maids came from a family
of one of the Eight Manchu Banners. They were chosen at set
ceremonies and had to be aged 13 to 17. While working in the palace,
the maids could gradually move from a lower to a higher position. At
the age of 25, they had to leave the palace. During the previous Ming
dynasty (1368-1644), however, once a maid was chosen to serve in
the palace, she was not permitted to leave, ever – a cruel rule.

INCREDIBLE!

EUNUCHS

MING EUNUCHS

All the imperial consorts lived in the Inner Court and were strictly forbidden to mingle with men (except the emperor and his children). Yet, there were some duties that couldn't be carried out by the maids. Therefore the men chosen to be servants in the Inner Court were castrated. These men were called eunuchs. This inhumane practice ended with the imperial dynasties.

# Elegant Maids in the Ming Palace

FACIAL FEATURES

LENGTH OF ARMS

MANNERS, VOICE, TEETH

THE FOREARMS CAN'T BE TOO SHORT.

MANNER OF WALKING

LENGTH OF LEGS

THE TOES CAN'T BE TOO LARGE.

The Ming love beauty.

Throughout the history of China, women often had to undergo a rigorous test in order to serve the emperor. During the Ming dynasty, good looks were the primary prerequisite for being chosen. Hands, arms, feet, and legs had to be in proper proportion, then the fairness of facial features was closely examined.

# Elegant Maids in the Qing Palace

VIRTUOUS AND GRACEFUL

**The Qing love virtuous and graceful women.**

THREE PAIRS OF EARRINGS
(YOU CAN'T WEAR JUST
ONE PAIR OF EARRINGS.)

To be chosen to serve as a maid in the Qing palace, a candidate had to be both beautiful and clever. Those who caught the emperor's eye would be promoted as imperial consorts. Life could be quite harsh for those who did not. They would serve as palace maids for many years until, in their twenties, they would leave the palace and pursue their own livelihood.

**FLOWERPOT-SOLE SHOES**
After founding the Qing dynasty, the Manchu women switched from their regular thick-heeled shoes to those with a small wooden stilt in the center under the soles. These were called "flowerpot-sole shoes." The narrow points of the shoes looked like the small and pointed bound feet of the Han women in China.

FIRST CLASS FEMALE ATTENDANT

IMPERIAL CONCUBINE

NOBLE LADY

SECOND CLASS FEMALE ATTENDANT

Do you want some tea?

YOUNG PALACE MAID

In imperial China, the practice of "one man with more than one wife" was officially accepted and carried out. An emperor would have an incredibly large group of consorts. Aside from the Empress, there were the Imperial Noble Consorts, Noble Consorts, Consorts, Imperial Concubines, Noble Ladies, First Class Female Attendants, and Second Class Female Attendants. They all lived in the Inner Court, and their sole duty was to serve and wait on their husband, the emperor, and to bear him children. Whoever gave birth to a child for the emperor was promptly rewarded with a promotion in her title and status.

In Chinese books and movies, the term "cold palace" refers to a fictitious place in the Forbidden City where consorts who were not in the emperor's favor were forced to live. Though the cold palace did

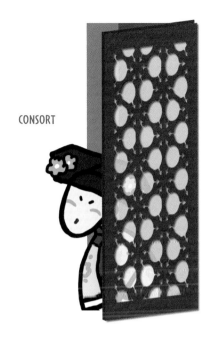

CONSORT

NOBLE CONSORT

IMPERIAL NOBLE CONSORT

not exist, there really were a good number of ladies who either were not in the emperor's favor or who got elbowed out by other ladies.

Emperor Kangxi of the Qing dynasty reproved the Ming imperial family for being too extravagant in keeping as many as 100,000 eunuchs and 9,000 palace maids in the Forbidden City. Some of the eunuchs became so powerful that they eventually caused the downfall of the Ming, while the palace maids ended up leading a miserable life of poverty and hunger, unknown to the world. With this hard lesson in mind, the Qing palace held austerity and frugality as its ideal. Yet at the height of the Qing dynasty, there were as many as 3,000 eunuchs and maids serving the imperial family in the palace. Can a "family" with 3,000 servants really be called austere or frugal?

LONELY CONSORTS

As there were no movie theaters, television sets, or computer games in the Forbidden City, the most popular entertainment was Chinese opera. At some point during the Qing dynasty, there were as many as 10 stages in the Forbidden City. Performances would be arranged by the Imperial Department of Entertainment. The troupes would most frequently present favorite scenes from well-known dramas.

THE EMPRESS DOWAGER

During birthday celebrations for emperors and empress dowagers, actors would be engaged to perform an elaborate full-length performance, called "Celebration of the Birthday of the Supreme Power." These performances could last from less than ten days to a month or longer. Emperor Qianlong of the Qing dynasty, known for being a good son, ordered a series of grand activities for the 60th birthday of his mother, Empress Dowager Chongqing. These activities covered a huge area, extending from the Forbidden City's West Prosperity Gate to Beijing's walls outside the Forbidden City. Lanterns were lit and banners of flowery gauze dazzled and fluttered everywhere. Different dramas and shows of song and dance were energetically performed. These fascinating sights must have filled the Empress Dowager's heart with happiness and pride.

**Hale and Hearty**

IMPERIAL PHYSICIAN

APPLYING ACUPUNCTURE TO A BRONZE FIGURINE

There were imperial physicians on call 24 hours a day for the emperor and his family. More than 400 herbal medicines were always in stock at the imperial pharmacy.

The emperors of the Qing led long lives, their average age of 53 years old was the highest in the history of China. The physical constitutions of the Qing emperors were stronger than those of previous emperors, and this certainly contributed to their longevity. This was also due to the skill of the imperial physicians.

There was a set standard for the food allotted to the emperor. The quantity of food that would be prepared for an emperor in one day was tremendous. The following is a list of the different kinds and amounts of food served. (1 jin equals a little less than 1 pound.)

fried or sautéed meat: 22 jin; meat for soup: 5 jin; lard: 1 jin; lamb: 2; chicken: 5; duck: 3; bok choy, spinach, parsley, celery, Chinese chives, etc: 19 jin; large turnips, water turnips, carrots, etc.: 60 pieces; cucumbers and winter melon: 1 of each; kohlrabi and dry water spinach: 5 of each; scallions: 6 jin; wine: 1/4 jin; sweet paste and salty paste: 3 jin of each; vinegar: 2 jin

Buns served with breakfast and supper: 8 platefuls, with 30 buns on each plate. Ingredients for the buns are as follows: first-rate white flour: 4 jin; fragrant oil: 1 jin; sesame seeds and bean paste: regular quantity; white sugar, walnuts, and black dates: 3/4 jin of each.

The quantity of beverages prepared daily was as follows: milk: 100 jin (if the 50 milk cows were able to provide 2 jin each that day); water from Yuquan: 12 pitchers; cream: 1 jin; tea leaves: 75 packs, with 1/8 jin in each pack.

An emperor, of course, could not possibly consume such a large quantity of food and drink each day. He would normally give the leftovers to his servants.

## Eunuchs: Imperial Food Testers

Serving a meal to the emperor was not easy. First the eunuchs had to serve the food by passing the dishes from one to another. Each dish had to be carefully tested to make sure it had not been poisoned. The emperor, for his part, had to be careful not to eat too much of one dish, even if he really liked it, because it might be more likely to be poisoned.

IMPERIAL PHYSICIAN

His Majesty's in perfect health!

PALACE CHAMBER POT

### Imperial Physician: Examining the Chamber Pot

The Forbidden City did not have flushing toilets like we do today. So the emperor and the imperial family used chamber pots, which were placed discreetly in backrooms and brought out by the eunuchs when needed. After the emperor went to the bathroom, the imperial physician would examine the color, shape, and hardness of what was in the emperor's pot, in order to diagnose the emperor's health.

WATCHING FOR
THE EMPEROR
TO COME OUT

Yes, yes, I hear you!

WAITING FOR THE EMPEROR TO COME BACK

Come Back to the Palace!

WAITING FOR THE EMPEROR TO COME BACK

A pair of stone columns, known as huabiao, stands inside and outside of Tiananmen Gate, at the entry to the Forbidden City. On each of the four columns is seated a small guardian creature. The two small beasts on the outside columns sit facing out onto Tiananmen Square. The other two, on the inside columns sit facing the palace. The small creatures are called "objects to ward off evil spirits." They symbolize protection from and the prevention of catastrophes. Though small in size, their postures are brave and ferocious, roaring fearlessly toward the heavens. Due to this, they are also called "Roaring Toward Heaven."

These four beasts have earned themselves two more names (one for each pair) that are quite amusing. The two facing away from the palace are called "Yearning for the Emperor to Hurry Back," for they sure look like they're eagerly waiting for an emperor, who has been gone for a long time on an imperial inspection, to return to the palace to take care of national affairs. As for the other pair, they are called "Yearning for the Emperor to Go on His Imperial Inspection Outside the Palace." These small beasts are telling the emperor not to lose himself in palace life, that he needs to show concern for the people by going out and conducting an imperial inspection. The emperor, whether leaving or returning, would be greeted by one of these loyal pairs.

71

# The 14 Confessions of Emperor Shunzhi

**CONFESSION 1**

I did not govern the nation well, which led to the suffering of my citizens.

**CONFESSION 2**

I was unfortunate to die before my mother and therefore unable to fulfill my duties as a good son.

**CONFESSION 3**

I was too young to properly mourn the death of my father for three years.

**CONFESSION 4**

I was cold and aloof to my paternal uncles, cousins, and nephews.

**CONFESSION 5**

I was too close to Han scholars and was distant from Manchu military staff.

**CONFESSION 6**

I was too demanding with my officials and was unable to overlook their shortcomings and make use of their talents, thus stifling their potential.

**CONFESSION 7**

I was too indulgent and lenient with officials who did not perform their duties and did not dismiss them when I should have.

**CONFESSION 8**

I neglected the problem of over-spending, which led to insufficient funding and supplies for the military. I gave orders for ministers and officials to cut their salaries yet did not cut over-spending in the palace, leading to complaints from my officials.

**CONFESSION 9**

I spent extravagantly on building luxury palaces, while disregarding the poverty and hardships suffered by my citizens.

**CONFESSION 10**

The funeral rituals and processions that I ordered for imperial consort Donggo were too costly and extravagant.

**CONFESSION 11**

I disregarded the lessons I should have learned from the Ming dynasty, and gave eunuchs too much power, leading to corruption.

**CONFESSION 12**

I engaged in too many pleasure-seeking activities and neglected to receive and exchange ideas with my ministers.

**CONFESSION 13**

I was too self-intoxicated and self-confident to heed the advice of my ministers, discouraging their counsel.

**CONFESSION 14**

I was aware of my wrongdoings, but did not correct them, which led to more wrongdoings.

## The Self-Criticism of Emperor Shunzhi (1644–1661)

Whenever the nation suffered from a natural disaster or political instability, a good emperor, or an emperor who tried to be a good one, would issue an imperial edict that was called a "self-criticism," which served as a confession to heaven, earth and all the people of the land, proclaiming: "All this is my fault. I'm the guilty one. So how about we let bygones be bygones!"

On the previous page is Emperor Shunzhi's self-criticism, confessing his past mistakes. This shows that an emperor was a unique creature. One day he's neglecting his responsibilities. The next he's taking all the blame!

How about we let bygones be bygones…

The ancients said it well: "The people of a country are like a river, and the emperor is a boat on the river. Whether the boat will sail smoothly or be capsized depends on the direction in which the boat is steered, with or against the currents." If life for the people is good, the emperor, Son of Heaven, will sit on his throne for a long time. In that case there's no need for this drama of self-criticism. Right? Don't you agree with me, Mr. Emperor?

## Historical Judgement:

# Imperial Diary, Posthumous Name, Temple Name

Whether an emperor was a good ruler was not determined by the emperor himself or by the opinions of his officials or people during his reign. A just evaluation could only begin after his death. After an emperor died, an honorary title would be given to him, which contained a commentary on his reign. An official committee in the palace determined this "Posthumous Name." For instance, the posthumous name for Emperor Kangxi has 25 Chinese characters. It reads, "the benevolent emperor whose fortune was blessed by Heaven, who accomplished unprecedented feats, who was steeped in both scholarly and military affairs, who was wise, philosophical, respectful, frugal, magnanimous, filially pious, sincere, trustworthy, moderate, and peaceful."

When an emperor died, he would also be given a "Temple Name" that would be inscribed on a tablet placed inside the imperial temple. The first emperor in a dynasty would have the title "Supreme Founder" or "Loftiest Founder," and the rest of the emperors would have the word "Ancestor" (zong) instead of "Founder" (zu) in their titles. There were, however, exceptions to this rule. The third Ming emperor, Yongle, had the temple name "Accomplished Founder" (Chengzu) and Emperor Kangxi, the second Qing emperor, was given the name "Sage Founder" (Shengzu) - all because of their memorable achievements.

During an emperor's lifetime, his spoken words and activities were recorded and later edited into a book titled "Imperial Diary." This was passed down as a historic record for the appraisal or critique of an emperor. In order to maintain objectivity, the emperor himself was not permitted to read or change these diaries. The only person who had the right to read them would be the mother of the emperor, the empress dowager.

OFFICIAL RECORDING AN
"IMPERIAL DIARY"

ACCOMPLISHED FOUNDER OF THE MING DYNASTY: **YONGLE**

SAGE FOUNDER OF THE QING DYNASTY: **KANGXI**

# THE EMPERORS OF THE MING AND QING DYNASTIES

The emperor says...

THEY MIGHT LOOK THE SAME,
BUT THEY ARE IN FACT
QUITE DIFFERENT.

*The emperors' names are listed as personal name / temple name / era name

### ZHU YUANZHANG / TAIZU / EMPEROR HONGWU*

Once a Buddhist monk, he became the founding emperor of the Ming dynasty, ruling China for 31 years, from 1368 to 1398. He set his palace in the city of Nanjing in the south.

## ZHU YUNWEN / HUIDI / EMPEROR JIANWEN

On the throne for four years (1399-1402), he angered the imperial princes (his uncles) when he attempted to take away their power. This led the Prince of Yan, Zhu Di, to take the capital by force. Jianwen ended up disappearing, with some reports stating that he burned to death, and others saying he fled to places unknown.

## ZHU DI / CHENGZU / EMPEROR YONGLE

He ruled for 22 years from 1403 to 1424 and moved the capital to Beijing. He ordered the writing and compilation of the Yongle Encyclopedia. He also gave orders to have the Forbidden City built.

### ZHU GAOCHI / RENZONG / EMPEROR HONGXI

On the throne for eight months in 1425, he was physically weak and grew obese as an adult, moving with difficulty. He died of illness in the Hall of Imperial Peace.

### ZHU ZHANJI / SIRE OF THE XUAN / EMPEROR XUANDE

On the throne for 10 years, from 1426 to 1435, Xuande liked hunting and archery, was a well-known gourmet, and became addicted to the game of cricket fighting. This earned him the nickname Emperor Cricket.

### ZHU QIZHEN / YINGZONG / EMPEROR ZHENGTONG & EMPEROR TIANSHUN

Zhu Qizhen reigned as emperor twice after his throne was snatched away from him for eight years. Thus he was the only emperor in the Ming Dynasty to have two reign titles, Zhengtong (1436-1449) and Tianshun (1457-1464).

JINGTAI VASE

### ZHU QIYU / DAIZONG / EMPEROR JINGTAI

He ruled for seven years from 1450 to 1457. Although Emperor Jingtai was on the throne for only a brief period, the Jingtai-style of cloisonné enamel, which was named after his reign title, became very famous.

Humph!

IMPERIAL NOBLE
CONSORT LADY WAN

## ZHU JIANSHEN / XIANZONG / EMPEROR CHENGHUA

Ruling for 23 years from 1465 to 1487, he had a lifelong infatuation
and romantic affair with Lady Wan, who was 19 years his senior.

## ZHU YOUCHENG / XIAOZONG / EMPEROR HONGZHI

He was on the throne for 18 years (1488-1505). Legend
has it that, after he was born, he went into hiding to avoid
being killed by the jealous Lady Wan. He met his father,
Emperor Chenghua, for the first time at the age of five.

Thoroughly rotten!

LEOPARD

Not so good, either!

PALACE CHAMBERMAID

PALACE CHAMBERMAID

## ZHU HOUZHAO / WUZONG / EMPEROR ZHENGDE

Zhengde sat on the throne for 16 years, from 1506 to 1521, during which time he would frequently sneak out of the palace and gallivant all over the country, visiting pleasure quarters and engaging in wild escapades. Sometimes he would be away from the capital Beijing for as long as a year. A hedonist through and through, he was so fond of leopards that he had a special hall built for the big cats named House of Leopards, where he would train them himself. He loathed staying in the Forbidden City and totally disregarded affairs of the state, leading to the decline of the Ming dynasty. In all, he was a poor excuse for an emperor.

## ZHU HOUCONG / SHIZONG / EMPEROR JIAJING

He ruled China for 45 years (1522-1566), during which time he indulged himself in wasteful construction projects, became a fanatic of occult Daoist teachings, and fell under the spell of fraudulent Daoist cult masters, whom he thought would help him become immortal. He was so despised by all others in the palace that he was almost killed by his own palace chambermaids when they staged a coup against him.

## ZHU ZAIHOU / MUZONG / EMPEROR LONGQING

During his six years on the throne (1567–1572), he learned and knew nothing about the affairs of state. Every time he held court and was asked by ministers for his opinion or decision, he would have the grand academician reply on his behalf. He would also keep completely silent when presiding over literary gatherings to discuss the classics.

## ZHU YIJUN / SHENZONG / EMPEROR WANLI

Wanli did not step out of the palace for over 20 years during the 48 years of his reign from 1573 to 1620! Yet he never tended to any official affairs; never presided over the sacrificial rituals to show reverence to Heaven and Earth; nor would he pay any respect to his ancestors. Furthermore, he flatly said no to holding court, to granting an audience to his ministers, to reading or responding to reports and letters of request from his ministers and officials, or to holding literary gatherings.

## ZHU CHANGLUO / GUANGZONG / EMPEROR TAICHANG

Taichang was on the throne for just one month in 1620. Physically weakened by overindulgence, he fell sick and was bed-ridden on the very day of his enthronement. He died soon afterward from an overdose of "elixirs" for immortality, prescribed to him by a Daoist monk.

## ZHU YOUXIAO / XIZONG / EMPEROR TIANQI

Ascending to the throne and ruling for seven years (1621-1627), he became emperor before he received any formal education. Born with a talent for carpentry, he was intensely attracted to the art of woodworking. He appointed a eunuch to be his Grand Counselor, the notoriously corrupt Wei Zhongxian, which led to the dismal decay of the monarchy.

**Alas! The great Ming Dynasty that lasted for 276 years has come to its end!**

**Attacking from the North**

## ZHU YOUJIAN / SIZONG / EMPEROR CHONGZHEN

As emperor for 17 years, from 1628 to 1644, he worked with utmost diligence all his life, managing the affairs of the declining dynasty. Austere and self-disciplined, he made a great effort to save the Ming dynasty, but in vain. This arduous and hardworking emperor came to a tragic end by hanging himself in Jingshan Park, outside the Forbidden City. With his death, the Ming dynasty ended.

## AISIN-GIORO NURHACI / TAIZU / TIANMING KHAN

He was khan for 11 years (1616-1626), fighting his way from beyond the northeastern territory of China to be the founder of the Qing dynasty.

## AISIN-GIORO HUANGTAIJI / TAIZONG / TIANCONG KHAN

Reigning for 17 years, from 1626 to 1643, he led his army to attack the Ming dynasty.

## AISIN-GIORO FULIN / SHIZU / EMPEROR SHUNZHI

Shunzhi ruled China as emperor for 18 years (1644-1661). He was the first Qing Dynasty emperor, ruling from the Forbidden City in Beijing. It remains a mystery whether or not he really died of smallpox.

**AISIN-GIORO XUANYE / SHENGZU / EMPEROR KANGXI**

Kangxi ruled for almost 61 years, from 1662 to 1722, the longest reign of any emperor in the history of China.

### AISIN-GIORO YINZHEN / SHIZONG / EMPEROR YONGZHENG

On the throne for 13 years (1723 to 1735), he came up with the device known as the "Box with the Name of the Heir Apparent," to prevent fierce struggles among the princes over whom would become the next emperor.

## AISIN-GIORO HONGLI / GAOZONG / EMPEROR QIANLONG

His 60-year reign (1736-1795) marked the height of the Qing dynasty's prosperity and strength.

**AISIN-GIORO YONGYAN / RENZONG / EMPEROR JIAQING**

Due to the long rule of his father, Emperor Qianlong, Emperor Jiaqing
spent an unusually long period of time studying before he finally
ascended to the throne. After becoming emperor, the Qing dynasty
began to show signs of its decline, including outbreaks of rebellion, all
of which Jiaqing found challenging to deal with. He reigned for 25 years,
from 1796 to 1820.

**AISIN-GIORO MINNING / XUANZONG / EMPEROR DAOGUANG**

He reigned for 30 years, from 1821 to 1850. When he was young, with extraordinary bravery, he fought off insurgents who attacked the palace. As emperor, he was conservative and frugal to the point of being stingy.

**AISIN-GIORO YIZHU / WENZONG / EMPEROR XIANFENG**

On the throne for 11 years (1851-1861), he was born prematurely, which resulted in poor health. During his reign, the Taiping Rebellion, aimed at overthrowing the Manchus, broke out.

## AISIN-GIORO ZAICHUN / MUZONG / EMPEROR TONGZHI

During the 13 years (1862-1874) of Tongzhi's reign, his mother, Empress Dowager Cixi, and the official empress dowager, Ci'an, would sit behind a curtain behind his throne and dictate to him how to govern as emperor. He was weak and powerless. Legend has it that his favorite activity was to frequent the saloons and opera houses in Beijing.

## AISIN-GIORO ZAITIAN / DEZONG / EMPEROR GUANGXU

During his 34-years-long reign (1875-1908), Empress Dowager Cixi continued to dictate how to rule. Guangxu endorsed and attempted to carry out a series of reforms in 1898. The Empress Dowager crushed this movement and then placed Guangxu under house arrest. Cixi was, in effect, the ruler of China for 48 years.

## AISIN-GIORO PUYI / EMPEROR XUANTONG

Ascending to the throne at the age of three, Puyi was emperor for three years, from 1909 to 1911, the last emperor of China. He was interested in Western culture, studied English, mathematics, world history, geography, and other subjects. Puyi was ordered out of the Forbidden City in 1924, and with his exit the imperial system of China officially ended.

## Our Expectations

The imperial system may have ended and the Forbidden City may have become the Palace Museum, but this history is as alive and exciting as ever. Thank you Mr. Emperor for telling us about your life. Now we wonder what it would be like if we were an emperor...

If you ask me, I'd say that a good emperor should...

_____

_____

_____

_____

## A Letter for You, in the Future

### Hello there, my friends!

As the Forbidden City has been preserved for 600 years, I hope you will also decide to preserve this little book. You can take it out and look at it whenever you want and, when you are older, you can take a look at it once more and remember these stories you read when you were young. Then it will be your turn to think about how you will re-tell these stories to the young children in your life.

Everything in the Forbidden City contains life. However our world has begun to change and become more unreal. The distance between people is greater and greater, the number of animal species is fewer and fewer, and plants are seen more often in parks, photographs, and on digital screens. The adjective "live" will soon need a new definition to be used in lives lived apart from it. So you see, my friends, everything in life deserves contemplation.

We all have something special we treasure. These things could be a story, a memory, or a valuable object. The Forbidden City, which has already been turned into a grand museum, is in itself a huge treasure. It is loaded with the most noteworthy moments of the Ming and Qing dynasties, containing tales and memories that are representative of the Chinese people, and valuable to all of humankind. All this is hidden inside one of the world's greatest palaces.

The truth is, as we are telling you that there were once more than 100,000 people leading their daily lives inside the palace (if the historical records are accurate), we are not completely certain exactly what it must

have been like to live there. According to an official report, in 2013 over 175,000 tourists visited the Forbidden City Palace Museum in one day. This number exceeds that of the world's most popular theme parks. For a palace, it is simply incredible.

Most of us will never become an emperor, an empress, a prince, or an imperial minister. It is also difficult for us to imagine life without technology. However, what we do know is that everyone, no matter who they are and which historical period they are from, experiences happiness and unhappiness, and possesses the hope to love and be loved. This hope has been passed on from generation to generation, until it dropped into our hands and we passed it on to you.

Now, my dear friends, we ask that you bring these hopes to the children of tomorrow.

I wish you all the very best!
**Chiu Kwong-chiu**
Design and Cultural Studies Workshop, Hong Kong

**We All Live in the Forbidden City**
What Was It Like, Mr. Emperor?
    Life in China's Forbidden City

Written by Chiu Kwong-chiu and Eileen Ng
Designed and Illustrated by Design and Cultural Studies Workshop
Translated by Ben Wang
Edited by Nancy S. Steinhardt

Original Book Design by Design and Cultural Studies Workshop Limited.
Book Design for the English edition by Arthur Gorelik & Design and Cultural
Studies Workshop Limited.

Managing Editors:
Michael Buening and Yuyang Li

Printed in Shenzhen, China by
Regent Publishing Services.

First edition, 2015
10 9 8 7 6 5 4 3 2 1

ISBN 978-0-9893776-6-9
Library of Congress Cataloguing-in-Publication Data is available under
LCCN 2015937329

Distributed by Tuttle Publishing
※ 364 Innovation Drive,
North Clarendon, VT 05759-9436

info@tuttlepublishing.com
www.tuttlepublishing.com

China Institute
※ 100 Washington Street,
New York, NY 10006

www.chinainstitute.org
www.walfc.org

This book and all **We All Live In The Forbidden City**-related
programming has been made possible through the generous support of the

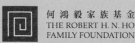
何 鴻 毅 家 族 基 金
THE ROBERT H. N. HO
FAMILY FOUNDATION

www.rhfamilyfoundation.org

## Books in the We All Live in the Forbidden City series

This is the Greatest Place! A Palace Inspired by the World of Small Animals

In the Forbidden City

Bowls of Happiness: Treasures from China and the Forbidden City

What Was It Like, Mr. Emperor? Life in China's Forbidden City

## About We All Live in the Forbidden City

In 2008 The Robert H. N. Ho Family Foundation collaborated with the Design and Cultural Studies Workshop (cnc.org.hk) in Hong Kong to create the We All Live in the Forbidden City (fc-edu.org) program. Using a contemporary voice and a variety of media formats, this program celebrates the Forbidden City and the study of architecture, imperial life, and Chinese cultural history in ways that are accessible, appealing, and relevant to children, parents, students, teachers, and the general public.

Working with China Institute in America, this program has now been brought to an English-language audience. Through four books, e-books, education programs, and a website, you will have the opportunity to learn about Chinese culture through this international icon. To learn more about the Forbidden City, WALFC, and to access games, activity guides, and videos, please visit www.walfc.org.

## About China Institute in America

Since its founding in 1926, China Institute has been dedicated to advancing a deeper understanding of China through programs in education, culture, business, and art in the belief that cross-cultural understanding strengthens our global community.

## Special Thanks

We at China Institute in America wish to express our gratitude to the many people who have worked with us on What Was It Like, Mr. Emperor? and the We All Live in the Forbidden City program. Ted Lipman, Jean Miao, and Wong Mei-yee of The Robert H. N. Ho Family Foundation for their support and guidance in shepherding this project to North America. Chiu Kwong-chiu, Eileen Ng, Selina Wong, and Ma Kin-chung of the Design and Cultural Studies Workshop and Alice Mak, Brian Tse, and Luk Chi-cheong for creating such wonderful books and for their advice and collaboration in developing the English language editions. Wang Yamin of the Palace Museum, and the editorial team of Palace Museum Publishing House, for their vital support and expertise since this program's inception in 2008.

We also wish to thank: Qi Yue, Li Ji, and Yang Changqing at the Palace Museum; Christopher Johns at Tuttle Publishing; Samuel Ing, Adrienne Becker, Jacqueline Emerson, Olivia Cheng, Stephanie Ridge, Andrea Christian, Ben Wang, Nancy S. Steinhardt, and Arthur Gorelik.